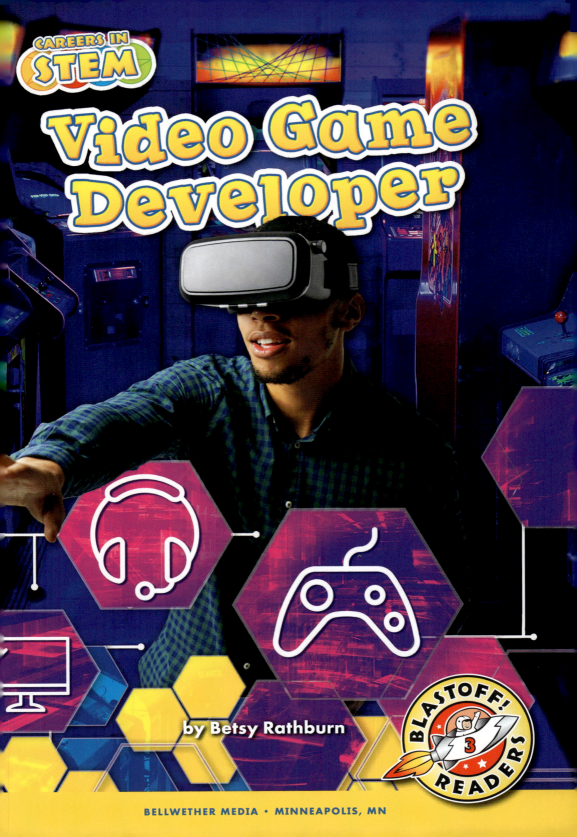

Video Game Developer

CAREERS IN STEM

by Betsy Rathburn

BELLWETHER MEDIA • MINNEAPOLIS, MN

Blastoff! Readers are carefully developed by literacy experts to build reading stamina and move students toward fluency by combining standards-based content with developmentally appropriate text.

LEVELS

Level 1 provides the most support through repetition of high-frequency words, light text, predictable sentence patterns, and strong visual support.

Level 2 offers early readers a bit more challenge through varied sentences, increased text load, and text-supportive special features.

Level 3 advances early-fluent readers toward fluency through increased text load, less reliance on photos, advancing concepts, longer sentences, and more complex special features.

★ **Blastoff! Universe**

Reading Level

Grade K

Grades 1–3

Grade 4

This edition first published in 2023 by Bellwether Media, Inc.

No part of this publication may be reproduced in whole or in part without written permission of the publisher. For information regarding permission, write to Bellwether Media, Inc., Attention: Permissions Department, 6012 Blue Circle Drive, Minnetonka, MN 55343.

Library of Congress Cataloging-in-Publication Data

LC record for Video Game Developer available at: https://lccn.loc.gov/2022036405

Text copyright © 2023 by Bellwether Media, Inc. BLASTOFF! READERS and associated logos are trademarks and/or registered trademarks of Bellwether Media, Inc.

Editor: Elizabeth Neuenfeldt   Designer: Andrea Schneider

Printed in the United States of America, North Mankato, MN.

Table of Contents

A New Game	4
What Is a Video Game Developer?	6
At Work	10
Becoming a Video Game Developer	18
Glossary	22
To Learn More	23
Index	24

A New Game

A video game developer writes **code** on a computer. He is making a new game.

The code will make a character jump and run. Soon, the game will be ready to play!

code

What Is a Video Game Developer?

smartphones

Video game developers create video games. Some make games for **smartphones**. Others make games for computers or **consoles**.

Developers do much of their work on computers. They **program** the games to work correctly.

console

programming a smartphone game

Developers work at small and large companies. Most go to offices. Some may work at home.

Famous Video Game Developer

Name: Eric Barone

Born: December 3, 1987

Birthplace: Los Angeles, California

Schooling: University of Washington Tacoma

Known For: Video game developer known for creating *Stardew Valley*

They work with many other people. They listen to others and share ideas.

At Work

graphics

Video game developers write code. The code tells the game what to do when a player presses a button.

Code also tells how to display **graphics** and when to play music.

Video Game Development in Real Life

mobile games

computer games

console games

Some developers make online games. Their code lets the game connect to the Internet. It connects people with other players!

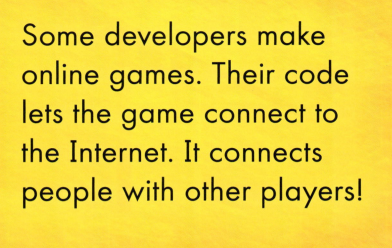

playing an online game

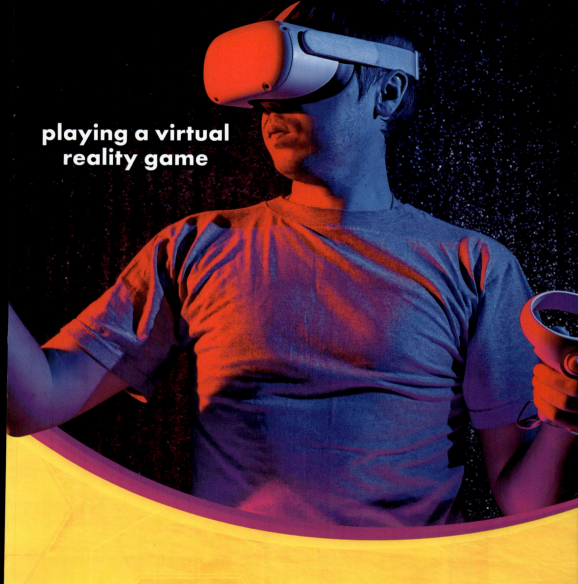

playing a virtual reality game

Others work with **virtual reality**. They program games that seem more real to players!

Developers work with other people. **Designers** tell them how the game should be played. Artists tell them how the game should look.

Developers help bring ideas to life!

artist

Developers test their code. They make sure the game works. They get **feedback** from their team.

They create **patches** to fix **bugs** or other problems. They make sure games are **secure**.

Using STEM

Science — study how computers work to make games

Technology — use computers to do work

Engineering — use code to create games

Math — use math to make code work

Becoming a Video Game Developer

Video game developers must be good with computers. They learn how to use **programming languages**.

Some go to college. They study computers. They also study math and science. Some study art, too.

programming language

Some video game developers get **internships**. They work with **expert** developers. They learn how video games are made.

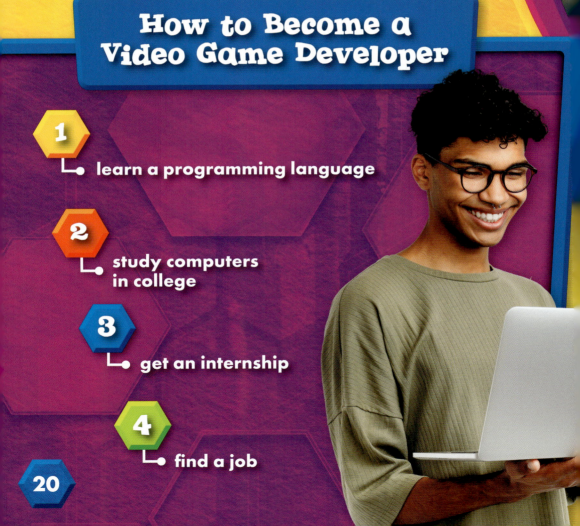

How to Become a Video Game Developer

1. learn a programming language
2. study computers in college
3. get an internship
4. find a job

Then, they get jobs. Their work gives us fun games to play!

Glossary

bugs—mistakes or problems in computer programs

code—programming instructions

consoles—game systems that connect to TVs to play video games

designers—people who plan how games should be played

expert—having a lot of knowledge or experience in something

feedback—information given about what can be done to make something better

graphics—pictures displayed on the screen

internships—programs in which people work at a job to gain work experience

patches—changes to a computer program to fix, update, or improve it

program—to create instructions for a computer to follow to complete a certain task

programming languages—ways of writing sets of instructions used to make computer programs

secure—not in danger of being damaged

smartphones—cell phones that let users connect to the Internet, use apps, and more

virtual reality—technology that uses sights, sounds, and player movement to make games more lifelike

To Learn More

AT THE LIBRARY

Dickmann, Nancy. *Ralph Baer: The Man Behind Video Games*. North Mankato, Minn.: Pebble, 2020.

Noll, Elizabeth. *Computer Programmer*. Minneapolis, Minn.: Bellwether Media, 2023.

Thiel, Kristin. *How Are Video Games Made and Sold?* New York, N.Y.: Cavendish Square Publishing, 2020.

ON THE WEB

FACTSURFER

Factsurfer.com gives you a safe, fun way to find more information.

1. Go to www.factsurfer.com.
2. Enter "video game developer" into the search box and click 🔍.
3. Select your book cover to see a list of related content.

Index

art, 18
artists, 14
Barone, Eric, 8
bugs, 17
code, 4, 10, 11, 12, 16
college, 18
companies, 8
computer, 4, 6, 7, 18
consoles, 6, 7
designers, 14, 15
feedback, 16
game, 4, 6, 7, 10, 12, 13, 14, 16, 17, 20, 21
graphics, 10, 11
how to become, 20
Internet, 12
internships, 20
math, 18
music, 11
offices, 8
patches, 17
people, 9, 12, 14

player, 10, 12, 13
program, 7, 13
programming languages, 18
science, 18
secure, 17
smartphones, 6, 7
study, 18
test, 16
using STEM, 17
video game development in real life, 11
virtual reality, 13

The images in this book are reproduced through the courtesy of: MBI/ Alamy, front cover (video game developer); Atmosphere1, front cover (background); Neveshkin Nikolay, p. 3; Vintage Tone, p. 4 (code); Gorodenkoff, pp. 4-5, 18-19, 20-21; fizkes, pp. 6-7 (smartphones); mkfilm, p. 7 (console); Konstantin Savusia, p. 7; Eric Barone/ Eric Barone, p. 8 (Eric Barone); Pixel-Shot, pp. 8-9; DC Studio, pp. 10-11; picsmart/ Alamy, p. 10 (graphics); Stoyan Yotov, p. 11 (mobile games); Terelyuk, p. 11 (computer games); StockImageFactory.com, p. 11 (console games); aslysun, p. 12 (playing an online game); Galina Sharapova, pp. 12-13; Frame Stock Footage, p. 14 (artist); C Studio, pp. 14-15; SeventyFour, pp. 16-17; mixtapedream/ Alamy, p. 18 (programming language); Inside Creative House, pp. 20-21 (video game developer); Chris Bardgett/ Alamy, p. 23.